A child's book of prayer

Compiled by Beth Sheeran

CLAREMONT

Published by the Penguin Group
Penguin Group (Australia)
250 Camberwell Road, Camberwell, Victoria 3124, Australia
(a division of Pearson Australia Group Pty Ltd)
Penguin Group (USA) Inc.
375 Hudson Street, New York, New York 10014, USA
Penguin Group (Canada)
10 Alcorn Avenue, Toronto, Ontario, Canada M4V 3B2
(a division of Pearson Penguin Canada Inc.)
Penguin Books Ltd
80 Strand, London WC2R 0RL, England
Penguin Ireland
25 St Stephen's Green, Dublin 2, Ireland
(a division of Penguin Books Ltd)
Penguin Books India Pvt Ltd
11 Community Centre, Panchsheel Park, New Delhi – 110 017, India
Penguin Group (NZ)
Cnr Airborne and Rosedale Roads, Albany, Auckland, New Zealand
(a division of Pearson New Zealand Ltd)
Penguin Books (South Africa) (Pty) Ltd
24 Sturdee Avenue, Rosebank, Johannesburg 2196, South Africa
Penguin Books Ltd, Registered Offices: 80 Strand, London, WC2R 0RL, England

First published by Penguin Group (Australia), a division of Pearson Australia Group Pty Ltd, 2004

1 3 5 7 9 10 8 6 4 2

Text copyright © Penguin Group (Australia) 2004
Photographs p. p. 18, 31, 39, 40, 64, 86 Corbis Images
p. p. 1, 2, 10, 14, 24, 28, 32, 36, 45, 53, 54, 58, 67, 76, 81 Getty Images
p. p. 17, 46, 68, 82 Photolibrary.com

The moral right of the author has been asserted

All rights reserved. Without limiting the rights under copyright reserved above, no part of this publication may be reproduced, stored in or introduced into a retrieval system, or transmitted, in any form or by any means (electronic, mechanical, photocopying, recording or otherwise), without the prior written permission of both the copyright owner and the above publisher of this book.

Cover design by Adam Laszczuk © Penguin Group (Australia)
Text design by Claire Tice © Penguin Group (Australia)
Cover photograph by Getty Images
Printed in China by Everbest Printing Co. Ltd

National Library of Australia
Cataloguing-in-Publication data:

Sheeran, Beth.
A child's book of prayer.
For children.

ISBN 0 7343 0615 6.

1. Children - Prayer-books and devotions. 2. Prayer-books.
I. Title.

242.62

www.puffin.com.au

contents

Prayers to start the day	1
Prayers of thanks	17
Prayers for the family	31
Grace	39
Prayers for the world	45
Prayers of praise	53
Prayers for help	67
Prayers for bedtime	81

This book has been written from my heart, and with the benefit of many years of experience as a mother, grandmother and religious educator. The collection includes traditional and modern prayers, collected from different sources, but all of them inspired by the voice of our Lord Jesus.

My hope is that I will be able to introduce children to the intimacy of the love of God. I believe that it is God's desire to be part of every child's life, and it is through prayer that children may communicate directly with Him.

God cares about everyone, no matter how young or old. He cares about every aspect of a child's life: school, family and friends. He is there for them through the life-changing events that touch children— death, loss, sudden change and trauma. God is their friend, helper and guide.

This book will offer comfort and hope to children, and help them to make sense of their world. Through prayer, children can explore their feelings, their fears, confusion, wonderment and joy.

Beth Sheeran

The Lord's Prayer

Our Father in heaven,

Holy is your Name.

Your kingdom come,

Your will be done on earth as it is in heaven.

Give us this day our daily bread,

And forgive us our sins as we forgive those who sin against us.

And lead us not into temptation,

But deliver us from evil.

For the kingdom and the power and the glory are yours,

Now and forever.

Amen

Thank you Lord, for this new day.
In my schoolwork and my play,
I hope you will be with me all day long,
When I play games and sing songs.
I hope all the happy things I do
Will make you, my Lord, happy too.
Amen

In the Bible we are told to love you best dear Lord,
Not to lie and not to steal.
To obey our mum and dad.
Not to want the things that other people have.
These are your commandments for us all.
Help me to obey them dear Lord.
Amen

Jesus Christ, who loves and takes care of us,
Please bless those people on the roads today.
Please watch over those driving cars and riding bikes.
Please watch over those driving buses and trucks.
Please bless the train and tram drivers to be safe.
Loving Father, please look out for everyone on the roads,
And help us to be careful when we cross the streets.
Amen

Loving heavenly Father,
Please be my guide through my day.
Watch over me during school and play,
So that I may be kind, loving and honest.
Amen

Dear Jesus, knowing that you are watching over me
Gives me strength each day.
Knowing that you love me,
Makes me feel warm and safe.
Thank you for loving me,
Even when I've been naughty and selfish.
Thank you for forgiving me
When I've been lazy and angry.
Please help me to be better,
For the next day, and forever.
Amen

Dear Jesus, I hope to do my best this day
So that I know it won't be wasted.
Every day is a precious gift.
For this I thank you.
Amen

Thank you Lord Jesus, for teaching us to forgive,
Just as you forgave those who hurt you.
Help us to remember how much you have forgiven us,
So that we are willing to forgive others.
Amen

Dear Lord, please bless my friends.
They are very important to me,
And make me laugh.
Please bless their school work
So they might do well.
Amen

God, who made all things on earth,
Who brought me into this world.
It is to you that I sit here and pray,
So that I will always strive
To be the best person I can.
Amen

God make my life a little light
Within the world to glow,
A little flame that burneth bright,
Wherever I may go.
Amen
    Matilda Barbara Betham-Edwards (1836–1919)

Lord Jesus, on this day,
Please watch over us as we play.
Help us to be kind and to play fair,
So that others may have their share.
Amen

Jesus, friend of little children,
Be a friend to me;
Take my hand and ever keep me
Close to Thee.
Amen
    Walter John Mathews (1853–1931)

Lord, be forever near me,
My master and my friend.
I shall not fear the battle
If you are by my side,
Nor wander from the pathway
If you will be my guide.
Amen
    John Ernest Bode (1816–74)

Dear Jesus,
I know you are with us always,
So please hear my call for your help.
Please guide me at school,
Especially through the hard times.
Amen

Lord Jesus, please help me
So that I may notice when others need my help.
Children who are alone, without friends or family,
My parents and teachers when they need a hand,
My friends when they are in trouble.
Please help me, Lord, to help others.
Amen

Prayers of thanks

We thank the Lord our God
For the world's beautiful things.
For the brightly coloured flowers
And the wonders that little creatures bring.
For the warm, shining sun,
And the glistening moon.
For all these wondrous things,
Who else can we thank,
Lord God, but you.
Amen

Dear Jesus,
It warms my heart to see people smile
Because of the gifts I give.
Thank you for being the one
Who taught me to be generous.
Amen

Dear God,
You have made me grateful
For all the wonderful things in my life.
Thank you for making me strong and healthy,
Thank you for my family and friends,
And thank you, most of all, for your love.
Amen

We give you thanks dear Lord Jesus,
For faith in a world where many walk in fear,
For friends in a world where many walk alone,
For food in a world where many walk in hunger,
And, most importantly, for your love and forgiveness.
Amen

Dear loving Father,
Thank you for the happiness
I feel in my play.
Help me to share this feeling
With others every day.
Amen

Thank you God, for your kindness on my birthday.
You have given me love from my parents,
Clothes and gifts so I may play,
And, most importantly, you have given me happiness,
So thank you, my Lord God, in every way.
Amen

Thanks to you, kind Father,
For my daily bread,
For my home and playthings,
For my cosy bed.
Amen

All good gifts around us
Are sent from heaven above;
Then thank the Lord, O thank the Lord,
For all His love.
    Matthias Claudius (1740–1815)

Thank you dear Lord Jesus that I can speak to you,
Whenever I am sad or glad, lonely or naughty too.
Thank you for being there to comfort and forgive.
To know that you are always near, means just everything.
Amen

Thank you dear Lord Jesus for Christmas.
For leaving such a wonderful place as heaven
To come to earth as a baby,
So that we can know you
As our Saviour and our Friend.
Amen

Prayers for the family

God our Father,
Thank you for my family,
For my parents, sisters and brothers,
For my grandparents, uncles, aunts and cousins.
Please keep them safe.
Amen

Dear Jesus, please hear my wish
That my mum and dad might live together again.
Please also hear my thanks
That I have a mum and dad.
Amen

Loving Father,
Please look after my grandparents.
We miss them dearly,
But we are happy because we know
They are with you in heaven.
Amen

Dear God,
Please help to make my family happy.
They are the most important thing in all the world.
Look after them with your love and care,
And let them be safe and free from harm.
Amen

Dear Jesus,
Thank you for my parents,
I love them in many ways.
They sometimes make me angry,
But really, that's okay!
I wouldn't be the person I am
If it wasn't for their love.
Amen

Heavenly Father, we ask that you bless this food,
So that we might have the strength to serve you.
Please send your blessing to those who have prepared it,
And please help those who go without
And are hungry in our world.
Amen

Please bless my daily food, dear Lord.
Make me strong of mind,
And kind of heart.
Amen

Thank you dear Lord Jesus for this beautiful meal.
Thank you Mum and Dad for shopping and cooking.
Amen

For what we are about to receive,
Lord make us truly thankful.
For Christ's sake.
Amen

Dear God, I want to thank you for this food,
And for our family and friends.
Amen

Dear God, bless this food to our bodies,
And bless us in your service,
In Jesus' name.
Amen

Prayers for the world

God our Father, creator of the world,
Help us to love one another.
Make nations friendly with other nations;
Make all of us love one another like family.
Help us to do our part to bring peace in the world and happiness to all people.
Amen

I pray to you Lord Jesus,
That our country may help
To make the world a better place.
Amen

Loving Father,
Please help bring peace to the world.
There is too much fighting
And not enough love.
Be our guide,
So that we might live
In harmony.
Amen

Sometimes the world seems like a frightening place.
We thank you God,
That you hold the world in your hands.
Your strength is all around and makes us safe.
Amen

The world is full of wonderful people,
Animals, plants and places.
All that you have made for us.
Help us to protect and care for each other
And the environment.
Amen

Dear Jesus, please help us to love one another,
So that we can be a part of bringing peace to the world.
Amen

Prayers of praise

We are blessed to have
Ears to hear the words of God,
Eyes with which to behold Him,
Feet to walk beside His footsteps,
Lips to sing His praise,
Hands to do His goodwill
And a heart with which to love Him.
Amen

We praise you Lord that even in times of sadness,
You are able to comfort and cheer us.
Amen

Dear God, thank you for creating our
Wonderful world and all that is in it:
The rich earth, the bright sky,
The warm sun and the blue ocean.
Everything that is good and beautiful.
Amen

We thank our Lord God
For our bodies that run and jump;
For our voices that laugh and sing;
For our little hands that work
To create beautiful things.
Amen

Thank You for the world so sweet.
Thank You for the food we eat.
Thank You for the birds that sing.
Thank You God for everything.
Amen

    Mrs E. Rutter Leatha

Our wonderful Father and our God,
Thank you for every good and beautiful thing
You have put into this world.
Fill our hearts with praise
For the wonderful people in our lives
Who give us joy and pleasure.
Help us to remember to praise you always.
Amen

Now thank we all our God
With hearts and hands and voices;
Such wonders he has done!
In him the world rejoices.
Amen

>After M. Rinkart 1586–1649
>Catherine Winkworth 1827–1878

Jesus, high in glory,
Lend a listening ear;
When we bow before Thee,
Children's praises hear.
    Harriet Burn McKeever (1807–1886)

All things bright and beautiful,
All creatures great and small,
All things wise and wonderful,
The Lord God made them all.

Each little flower that opens,
Each little bird that sings,
He made their glowing colours,
He made their tiny wings.

The purple-headed mountain,
The river running by,
The sunset, and the morning
That brightens up the sky.

The cold wind in the winter,
The pleasant summer sun,
The ripe fruits in the garden,
He made them every one.

He gave us eyes to see them,
And lips that we might tell
How great is God Almighty,
Who has made all things well.

Cecil Frances Alexander (1818–1895)

Dear Jesus,
When I feel scared
My tummy feels full
Of tiny little butterflies.
I hope you will hear
When I ask for your help
To make me brave
And not scared any more.
I'm glad to know
That you are by my side.
Amen

Help me dear God to follow your commandments.
Not to use bad words or to tell lies.
To do as my parents tell me.
Not to steal.
Not to desire what another person has.
Help me to love and serve you with all my heart.
Amen

Help me dear Jesus, to treat other people
As I would like them to treat me.
Because You have told us in the Bible:
To do to others as we would like them to do to us.
Amen

Father, be our strength in hours of weakness,
In our wanderings, be our guide;
Through endeavour, failure, danger,
Father, be there at our side.
    Love Maria Willis (1824–1908)

Dear Lord, when I feel angry and I talk to you about it,
You take the anger away.
You help me to see things differently,
To see things from another person's point of view.
Amen

Dear God, sometimes I feel as though
I have no friends, only enemies.
Help me to be loving to those people who are unkind to me,
Help me to remember that you love me always.
Amen

Dear God, you have angels everywhere
To protect and care for me.
They are with me every minute of the day and night.
I love you Jesus.
Amen

Jesus, at times I am afraid and scared of the dark,
But you are always with me, wherever I am.
Knowing you are there
Helps me to feel calm and peaceful and safe,
And I don't need to be scared at all.
Amen

Dear God, I really miss my grandpa,
I wish that he was still here and that he had not died.
Please look after Grandpa now that he is in heaven with you.
I loved him so much.
Amen

Dear God, why does everything have to change?
I liked my life the way it was before.
I need you to be with me now that my life is suddenly different.
You are the only one that does not change.
Amen

Dear Jesus, our family is moving to a new house.
I don't want to leave my friends or my school
And I am afraid I will be lonely
Without the people and things that are familiar.
Please help me to remember that you will always be with me,
Helping me to find new friends,
And helping me to enjoy my new house and school.
Amen

Dear God, sometimes I feel all alone.
I think that no one really understands me or knows how I feel.
You know me better than anyone,
I can talk to you any time of the day or night.
You are always there for me.
Amen

Sometimes I think no one can help me,
My homework is so hard.
Please be my guide, Lord,
So I can do my best
And make my teacher proud.
Amen

As the sun quietly sets
And the birds become calm,
I rest my weary body
And ask you, dear Lord,
To keep me from harm.
Amen

Jesus, tender shepherd, hear me;
Bless Thy little lamb tonight;
Through the darkness be Thou near me;
Keep me safe till morning light.
Amen
    Mary Duncan (1814–1840)

Thank you Lord, for your forgiveness,
For forgiving me every day;
For when I do the wrong thing,
And for the things I say.
Help me Lord to forgive others.
Please give me the strength
So that I might be like you one day.
Please hear me as I pray.
Amen

Dear Jesus,
I ask for forgivness.
Today I did something wrong,
And then lied so I wouldn't get the blame.
Tomorrow, with your help,
I will do the right thing.
Amen

Though I cannot see you,
I am grateful, Lord, that you are so close.
Though I do not tell you my thoughts,
You know what I am thinking
And what I am feeling.
I thank you for listening to me
And for your forgiveness.
Please stay with me always.
Amen

Gentle Jesus, meek and mild,
Look upon a little child,
Pity my simplicity,
Suffer me to come to Thee.
Amen

    Charles Wesley (1707–1788)

Lord Jesus, please forgive my angry words,
I don't mean what I say.
Please forgive my petty moods,
Which spoil my happy day.
Please forgive the mess I make,
And leave all over the floor.
Please forgive my unfinished dinner,
And my forgotten chores.
I hope you'll forgive my selfish ways,
And those times when I sin.
Help me be a better person,
When the next day begins.
Amen

As the bright moon shines,
And the stars give their light,
We ask for God to bless us
And to watch over us all.
Amen